The World and Beyond: Chapbook of Poetry Book 1: Four Seasons

The World and Beyond: Chapbook of Poetry Book 1: Four Seasons

Caroline Elizabeth Coleman Vaile

"POETRY THAT EXPLORES THE STRENGTHS AND WEAKNESS OF THE MIND, THE DEPTHS OF THE HEART, THE MYSTERIES OF THE SOUL, DEEP EMOTIONS, HARNESSED SENSATIONS, THE NATURAL WORLD, AND THE EXPLORED THEORIES OF THE UNIVERSE."

Caroline Vaile Publishing

First Edition

10 9 8 7 6 5 4 3 2 1

Mena, Arkansas© All rights reserved

Published in United States of America

ISBN: 979-8-9861911-2-6 (Paperback)

ISBN: 979-8-9861911-3-3 (EPUB)

Illustrations, Interior Design, Book Cover Design by Caroline E. Vaile

2022 Caroline E. Vaile

Table of Contents

BLUSH

A fresh and frozen vibrant riddle,

A trivial note with sensational rhythm,

A fragrant rosy blush and bitter brew,

A brilliant glance of baby blue,

A fine shine and wide-eyed refuge,

A stringing string strum on a folk singers
fiddle,

Pressed loosely to a a firm cheek sleek
and mild,

And by and by your endless smile.

IDLE RESERVATIONS

I followed you around while you idly
watched the moment pass,

Struck by the moment you appeared
bewildered in,

The earth around your feet seemed to
move too fast,

Captured by the moment and persuaded
by a whim.

I couldn't be the rock that tapped at your
feet,

Smothered by the leaves that covered
you,

The wind would howl and stifle your
grief,

Swallowed by your refuge that guided
you.

I borrowed the path that pressed your
feet to the breeze,

Carried away with your clever
reservations,

The leaning you perched was meant for
the trees,

Starved for your silence and
preservation.

SENTIMENT

A

Sentiment.

A voluntary notion,

capable of extending expression

that fills a void. Warm and welcoming
for most.

The least most present often occupies the
most. An inspiring thought

creates memories, that creates
friendships, that brings people together.

Places are created, relationships are
made, families are started with just a few
simple and thoughtful words.

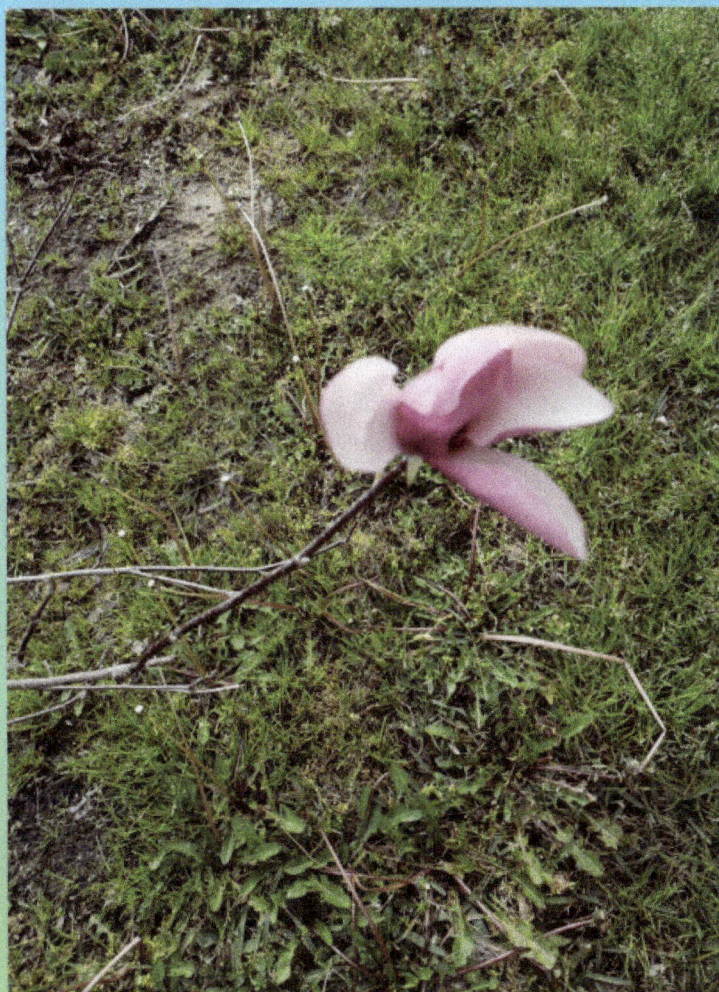

AN INVENTORS QUERY

Near as a nights time so fair footed he
traveled as far as the scent of pine

In his drift he tipped his hat made way
with his ease in his gentle stride

Kept like a striking match whose flint
secured his place amongst the call of the
Whippoorwill

On the horizon his toil blazed long into
night into the fight of his days and on
still

Love were tears that fell long to his feet
as were the emotions like anchors that
held him

Afraid of his ways the loss that turned
into his days that smuggled his longing
to heal them

Time was his avenue that drove him hard
to his virtue

Every page he turned swept away the
wind between him and kisses the wind
blew

Silence so mysterious drew his
attentions like a riddle

Lighting up life with the healing sands
of time and the means to have them

Almighty his God spoke magic in the air
into his ear through his mothers fears,
segit.

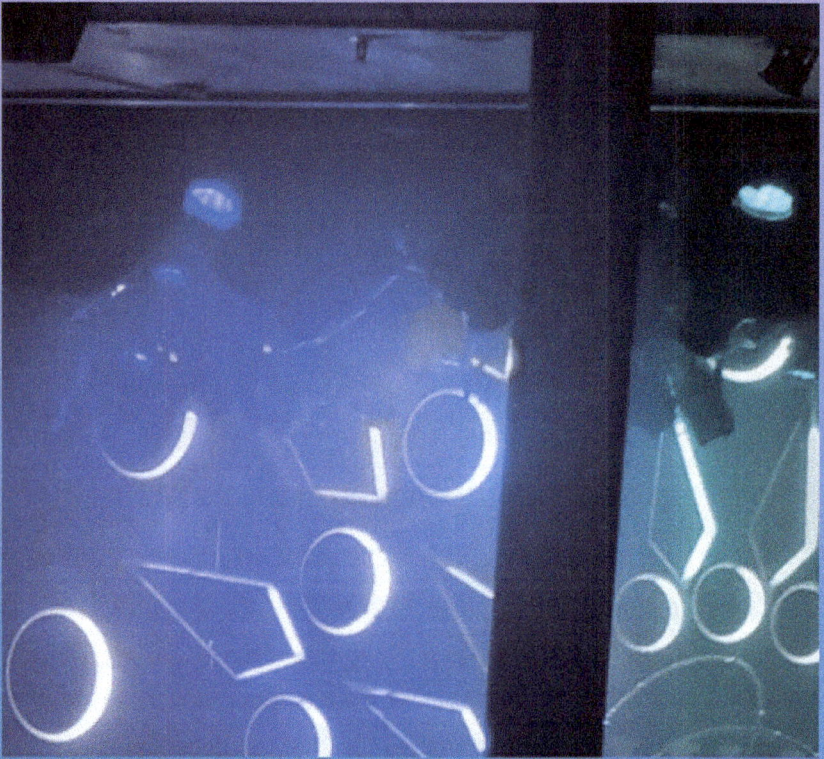

GRAVITY

I stand strong again in this pursuit with
my imagination far reaching

The colors of the sky deep in blue are
carried by the hills

My nose is stuck out as far as the scent
of warm bread drifts

And in the streets the cars move faster
than my dreams

Beautiful is the sound of quiet as you are
thinking big

As strong as my ambitions are as strong
as the race to catch them.

FREE WILL

Loud tears in the moonlight, soft rain
drops sound

Run into the night, quietly sit there

Sing a long song, breathe gently no
one hears

Darkness hides in the night, daylight
rings loud

Run run from the night, light steps tip
toe round

Break far from the chains, easy are your
fears

Smile greet each day, grin and bear the
years

Stroll stroll with the light, wait for new
days found

Cheerful cries the noise, humbled were
the days

Rise of shoes stomping echo, slowly
stepped

Freedom moved swiftly, folded hands
prayed tight

Joy brought the light, calming the newly
saved

Lifted by strength, although they all had
wept

LONG SO TRAVELED

Long so traveled and swept away

You came to me from a world of mystery

Fevered as the sun and windy as the
storms on the bay

On my swing so patiently resting,
singing, with the sway

You there from beyond the vast sea,
beckon me

Long so traveled and swept away

I long awaited for just a sign, a bellow,
everyday

You drifted closer and closer and closer
it seemed

Fevered as the sun and windy as the
storms on the bay

I opened my eyes to see stormy clouds
and deep shadows of gray

You master of the wind, master of the
storms, master of the sea

Long so traveled and swept away

I envisioned the moment you would
head my way

You captured my heart took my breath
and set me free

Fevered as the sun and windy as the
storms on the bay

I grieved as many who await their love
to come home to stay

Fevered as the sun and windy as the
storms on the sea

Long so traveled and swept away

Dying

Many a man far reaching, the sands of
time call

Raptured, into the empty, endless, abyss

You are as to the sea as vast as time gets

I am your endeavor...you harvester, you
charter, you dweller

Please carry me in your whimsy and
proud grasp

Your query is seizing, harnessing, and
slowly squeezing

I am in the midst of it all as you are
careful, daunting, and stealing

My time has burdened you, taunted you,
called to you...perhaps

Your refuge of song, step, and dance is
where I belong

Stuck in the embrace of a silent savior
who knows only my dismay

I am betwixt in this ascension, this
transition, this change

It is with you that I have secured my
days, my strength, my God

SOUL-TIES

Follow me my faithful friend

Our journey belongs to us

Wiseman's tale around the bend

Nighttime is bright with stardust

Joyful lover faithful friend

Daylight shines and glorifies

Defined by our journeys end

Riddled and rhymed bound soul-ties

FAITHFUL

He of little faith

Unrighteous anger is sin

He said its finished

SUMMONED

Trumpets in my dreams command

Steps the summoned to gather

Huddled masses changed by light

Traveling band through times charter

DON'T FALL IN LOVE

Just don't fall in love

Don't look at me with loving eyes and
open ears

Don't read my poems and expect them to
take you somewhere

Don't let my words embrace your
thoughts

Don't feel my words and take my pain

Don't you dare fall in love this way

Don't hear my story, not this way

Just don't dare fall in love

Don't sympathize or agonize or feel my pain

Don't let me whisper words in your ears

Don't let me twist up your emotions with my thoughts

Don't read my poems and run off somewhere

Don't think that I write to take you somewhere

Don't follow me to the depth, even I don't know the way

Don't let me misinterpret your thoughts

Just don't fall in love

Don't hear the singing of my swallows
in your ears

Don't wander the streets at night to ease
the pain

Don't copy me not every word I say in
pain

Don't slam the door and go somewhere

Don't blame me when my words burn
your ears

Don't hate me when I lead the way
Just don't dare fall in love

Don't let me impress you with my
thoughts

Don't let me change your mind or your
thoughts

Don't let me hold your hand to hide the pain

Just don't fall in love

Don't let me kiss you and take you somewhere

Don't lean on me and and learn love this way

Don't let me whisper sweet nothings in your ear

Don't lay your head on my shoulder and cry in my ear

Don't give me a way to control your thoughts

Don't spend a moment of your time this way

Don't fall helplessly in my words to steal your pain

Don't let my words guide your heart somewhere

Just don't fall in love

Don't steal my love and call it your pain

Don't just stand there, go somewhere

Just don't fall in love

AGAIN I TRUST

I want to see you again

I want to hold you again

Again we reach out

Again we connect

Connect with the undefined

Connect to a few heavy moments

Moments we should not leave waisted

Moments we need to express

Express our sympathy

Express our regrets

Regrets are meaningless

Regrets are measured

Measured are our days

Measured are our lives

Lives rock sway in the wind

Lives like matches strike flames

Flames burn on timber

Flames burn through the night

Night brings solace

Night brings change

Change suffers

Change Stirs

Stirs mix

Stirs blend

Blend life's colors into one

Blend life's emotions

Emotions create definitions

Emotions drive life

Life challenges

Life brings love

Love transcends

Love redefines

Redefines our conscious

Redefines our heart

Heart is made for healing

Heart breeds the lonesome

Lonesome doves are still a pair

Lonesome people still exist

Exist not only to live

Exist to find Joy

Joy brings laughter

Joy finds happiness

Happiness fills a void

Happiness leads me to you

You give me purpose

You teach me to trust

Trust makes me want to see you again

Trust makes me want to hold you again

Again

You

FOUR SEASONS

Dandelion pressed stressed to the ground

The stored blown seeds broke free from
their pods

Wagon wheels stroll the ground with
crackling sounds

To be stifled by the radiant brace of the
sun

High waters and stormy seas make
slashing sounds

Sun cast shadows bounce off of the
ground in the shapes of clouds

And fresh magnolia blooms are found fit
for the bees now

Swept away by the fleeting and brisk
wind gusts

Blown far into the night battered leaves
fall to the ground

Lonely are the trees whose hearts beat
different shades of brown

As pale as the moonlight shinning down
snow falls about

Firelight warms and nestles like a touch

Fire flies and long goodbyes in tall fields
bound

Fragrance and laughter arise throughout
the town

MIDNIGHT RIDER

It isn't a case of things that go bump in
the night

The wind started to whistle, the floors
did creek,

A storm fast approached the terminator
line

My front porch swing hit jabbed a porch
beam

And the wild wind gust blew open my
shutters

There was a flash, a flutter, a
flicker...and then lights out

I was longing for the olden day's and
candle light

A glowing oil lamp night or reason to sit
by a warm fire

My porch door slams wildly, thrusting,
wind rustling

Rain kept whipped hit the tin roof with
raging force

Louder than the sound of a pounding and
beating heart

A wreckage of branches strike tumbled
the shed

Emergency sirens sounded loudly

There was a clink, a clash, a clatter...and
the window was blown out

Hours past huddled bundled in blankets
in the old claw tub

Silence and disturbance replaced the
dew dropped oak leaves

As grim as the forecast hence the day
was subdued

Debris thrown strew along the sidewalk
and street

Gentile efforts did stake claim to take
back the day

There was a wane, a wince, a
weather...and much fallout

TROPICAL SUNSHINE

Tropical sunshine your fruit and feather
be

Brilliant blue with sunset hues and
poised claws

Voyager of time and treasures of the
trees

Ancient settler whose perch leg beams

Bring to me your delightful travelers
song

Tropical sunshine your fruit and feather
be

Marigold brightness whose wings span
long

Wind and flight far carry thee

Brilliant blue with sunset hues and
poised claws

Sage Avarian your wisdom transcends
the seas

Mercy from your bird song sings a
joyful sound

Voyager of time and treasures of the
trees

BEYOND THE TREES

Sleep leaning whispering hollow

Tall and deeply swaying gallow

Can I follow you through into the deep

A leafy forest peak

Your timber's are tall and peering

Reaching is your pillar's viewing

Mindful perching hasten a restful hunt

Sun bathing travelers brush

What lies beyond your endless bend

Beyond your sheltered piney den

Many days travel through your dusty
woods

Proudly stood one afoot

REJOICE

Humbly bumbled like little bee's

Grow as big as the tree's

Come gather fruits and nuts

Grow as big as the tree's

Find your strength in natures breeze

Grow as big as the tree's

Shine bright and play in the sun

Grow as big as the tree's

Lift your love and spread your wings

Grow as big as the tree's

DAY IN A LIFE

I could sit here all day

I could spend my days turning pages

I could strum my strings dreaming of
new places

I could sit here all day

I could spend my days turning pages

I could wait for the hours to pass me by

I could paint a picture of a sunset sky

I could spend my days turning pages

I could wait for the hours to pass me by

I could dream of dreamy rainbows

I could take long drives down winding roads

I could wait for the hours to pass me by

I could dream of dreamy rainbows

I could sway with the wind on sunny beaches

I could pan for gold in a waterfalls creek

I could dream of dreamy rainbows

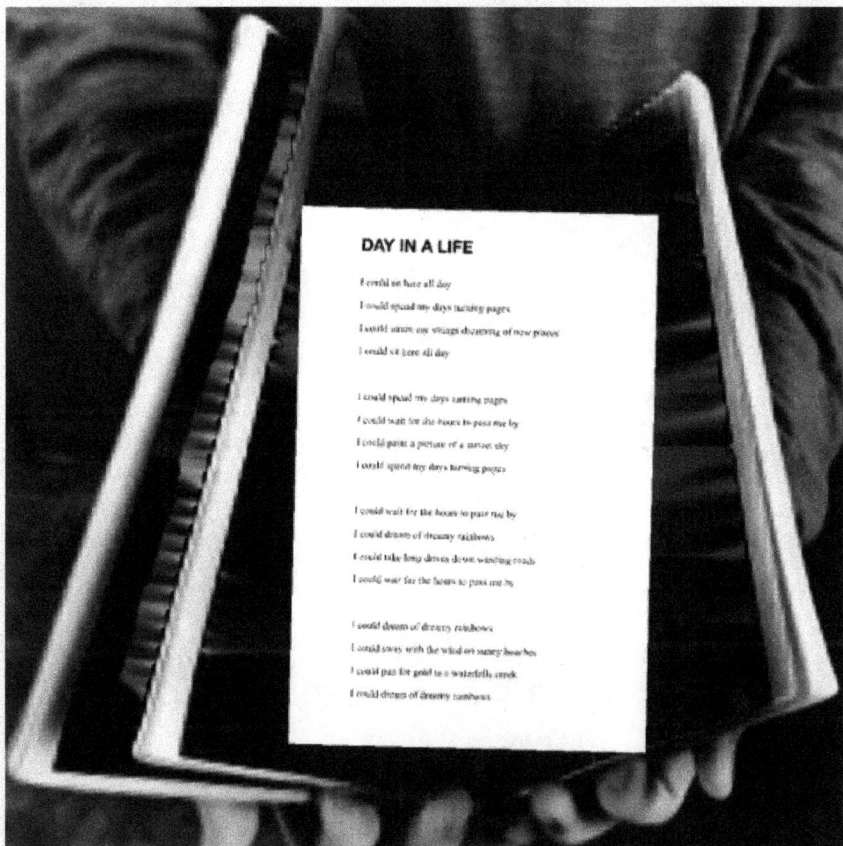

DAY IN A LIFE

I could sit here all day
I could spend my days turning pages
I could stare out windows dreaming of new places
I could sit here all day

I could spend my days turning pages
I could wait for the hours to pass me by
I could paint a picture of a sunset sky
I could spend my days turning pages

I could wait for the hours to pass me by
I could dream of dreamy rainbows
I could take long drives down winding roads
I could wait for the hours to pass me by

I could dream of dreamy rainbows
I could sway with the wind on sunny beaches
I could pan for gold in a waterfalls creek
I could dream of dreamy rainbows

SANDS OF TIME

Time as it is and time be as it may

May the roll tide wave and waves crash
shorelines

Shorelines drift heavy winds and salty
sting

Day in the sun and just another day

Day's warm touch and rays of beaming
sunshine

Sunshine reveals and bursts of light
bounce fling

Moments to spare and more coming your
way

Way blasts the winds about and breeze
turbine

Turbine and polish the stones in the
spring

Foregoing and previse ancient display

Display turns the hour glass and throws
time

Time changes all kinds and everything

Spun notes sailing and freshly molded
clay

Clay like time molds and sunset brings
the night

Night turns into day and galaxy gleams

TASTY

Tasty

Cold and Stinging

Creamy Ice Creamy dream

Chocolate and Vanilla please

Tasty

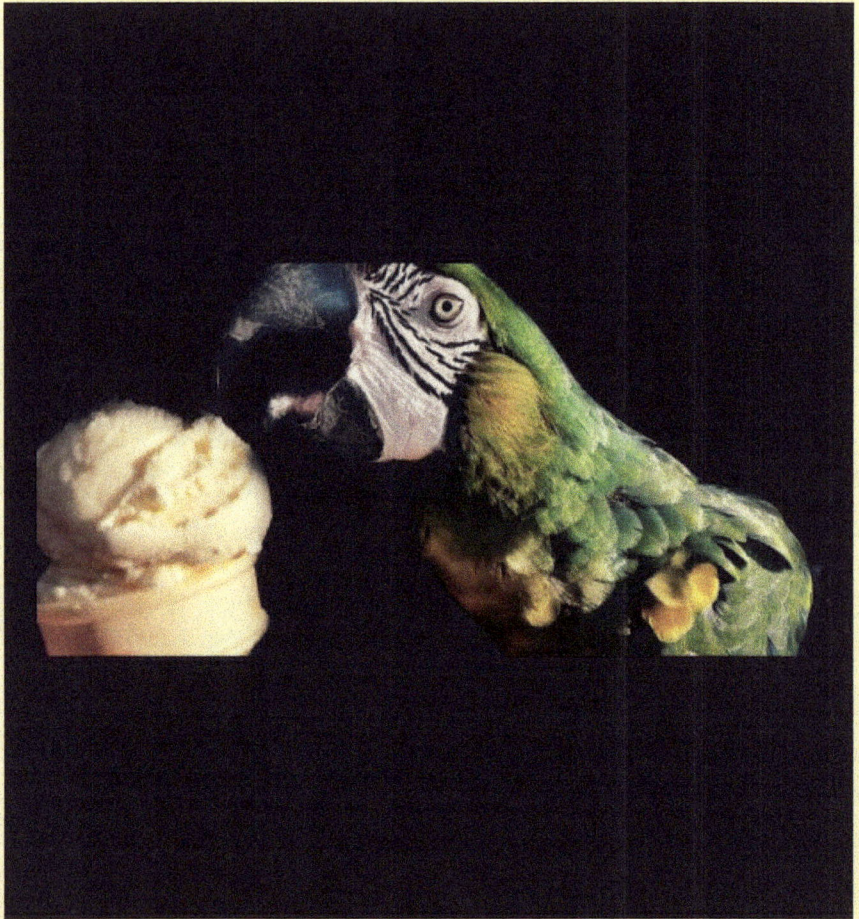

YOUR LOVE

Your love depends on the weather

A forecast of changing treasure

Forever dreaming

Clever mystery

Whenever

Together

Your love is an endless journey

Destination unknown to me

Looking for reasons

Searching the seasons

Needs depend

Exploring

Your love is moving and transcends

Drifts weightlessly shifting within

Becomes different

Sometimes a brilliant

Experiment

Enchantment

CELESTINE

Are you an angel?

Your heavenly presence and baby blue

Poised and polished sparkling blue

Sleek and radiant diamond like blue

Are you an angel?

MY CHRISTMAS BIRD

Merry, merry, cheer, and beaky bell

A truly holly and jolly

Heavenly creature does tell

Yuletide songs sings greetings

Angels in waiting

Christmas polly

Chime your sweet

Noel

Chime

ABOUT THE AUTHOR

Caroline Elizabeth Coleman-Vaile (B.1978)

Caroline Coleman Vaile (b. 1978) resides with Bill Vaile, and her son Ryan in one of the many beautiful mountain valley's in Arkansas, where they care for their rescued animals.

Caroline worked as an Administrative Assistant in Business Operations for pharmaceutical and retail companies. Administrated and managed a DEA Controlled Substance Unit and filled pharmacy orders for Animal Healthcare for 20 Years, and before that she was a Nurses Aid caring for the elderly in nursing homes.

She has spent the last eight years studying Genealogy and the Hungarian language, as her Winbauer Heritage from Bavaria, Germany, her Deak Heritage who is Austria-Hungarian from Budapest, her Coleman Heritage from Mango, Essex, England, her Giffin Heritage from Southend Parish, Argyllshire Co, Kildavee, Scotland mystifies and interests her.

Caroline is the Author, Illustrator of 2014 *Avant-grade: Four Seasons* VAu001192990, the, 2016 *Avant-grade Science of Religion* VAu001247003, and of 2012 *Passenger Tones* abandoned patent application US2012/0276935A1. (Abandoned due to lack of funding)

Her hobbies include writing poetry, patent writing, other technical writing, data mining for new invention material compounds, and gardening. Her latest work is *Satanic Warfare: Tactics of the Demonic* published a long side of Bill Vaile and Monica Koldyke Miller. She expresses that one of her most profound beliefs is that Nano Tubes and Teslaphoresis are the building block for the future of all materials and the key to time travel! She considers herself a *'Jill of all trades'* and expresses *"it's better to try and fail then to never try at all."*

www.ingramcontent.com/pod-product-compliance
Lightning Source LLC
Chambersburg PA
CBHW071929020426
42331CB00010B/2786